CCSS **Genre** Exposit...

Essential Question
What can you discover when you look closely at something?

Secrets of the Ice

by Rachel Hayward

Chapter 1
The Properties of Water......................2

Chapter 2
Snow and Ice................................6

Chapter 3
Looking Closely at Ice 10

Respond to Reading........................15

PAIRED READ Super-vision 16

Glossary/Index..............................19

STEM Focus on Science 20

Kenneth G. Libbrecht

❄ CHAPTER 1 ❄
The Properties of Water

What is transparent, wet, and flows out of a faucet? What is cold, hard, and floats in a glass? What is invisible and suspended in the air?

The answer is water. Water has three different **states**. It can be a liquid (water), a solid (ice), or a gas (water vapor or steam). Water is found in rivers and oceans. Ice is found high in the mountains and in the polar regions. Water vapor is all around us in the air.

(bl) Brand X Pictures/Punchstock (br) 81a/age fotostock

Water is unique because it's the only substance that naturally occurs on Earth as a liquid, a solid, and a gas.

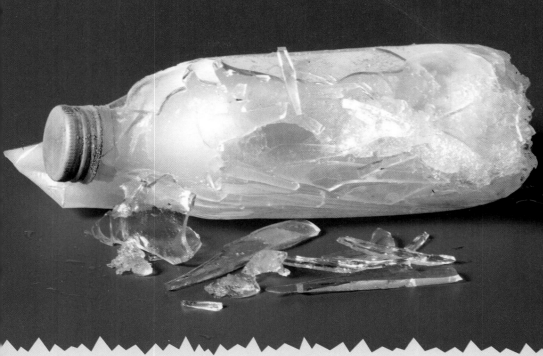

Water has other special qualities. Water is a **solvent**. When it is a liquid, substances such as salt, sugar, oxygen, and carbon dioxide dissolve easily in it.

When water cools to 32 degrees Fahrenheit, it freezes and becomes ice. Most substances shrink when they freeze, but water expands. If you freeze a glass bottle full of water, the water will expand and the bottle will break.

When water occurs as a gas, or vapor, it is usually invisible. Air with a large amount of water vapor feels humid and sticky.

(tc) Martyn F. Chillmaid/
Photo Researchers, Inc. (bl)
Jupiterimages/Thinkstock Images

Although the amount of water on Earth and in the atmosphere stays the same, it changes from one state to another. Water constantly moves around Earth. This process is called the water cycle.

The sun provides the energy for the water cycle. When the sun heats water, it changes the water from a liquid into a gas. This change is called **evaporation**. Some of the water in lakes, rivers, and oceans evaporates and becomes water vapor. The vapor rises up into the **atmosphere**.

As the vapor rises into the atmosphere, it cools. This makes it **condense** back into a liquid. The water vapor forms tiny water droplets when it condenses, which make clouds and mist.

Ingram Publishing/SuperStock

When the sun evaporates water from a lake, the vapor can appear as mist.

When the droplets of water become a cloud, they join together with other droplets. This makes them heavy, and they fall back to Earth as rain, hail, sleet, or snow. The kind of precipitation that falls depends on the temperature.

The water that returns to Earth collects in streams, rivers, or the ground. Then it's heated by the sun, and the cycle begins all over again.

As water circulates around Earth, it picks up other substances from the environment. Even when it changes from a liquid into ice or vapor, dust or other substances that are in the water stay in it. By closely examining the substances in the water, we can get information about our planet.

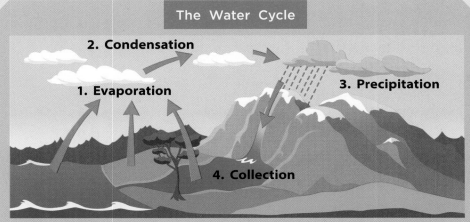

The Water Cycle

2. Condensation

1. Evaporation

3. Precipitation

4. Collection

1. **Evaporation**—Water is heated by the sun and turns into vapor.

2. **Condensation**—The vapor cools and turns back into a liquid.

3. **Precipitation**—The liquid falls back to Earth as rain, hail, sleet, or snow.

4. **Collection**—The water collects in streams, rivers, or the ground.

CHAPTER 2

Snow and Ice

Snow forms when water vapor condenses into droplets and then cold air freezes the droplets into ice crystals.

As each crystal grows, it sticks to other ice crystals and forms a group of crystals. When the group of ice crystals becomes heavy enough, it falls to Earth as a snowflake.

Ice crystals grow in many different shapes. The shape depends on the temperature in the atmosphere when the crystal is forming. If it's very cold (around 5 degrees Fahrenheit), the crystals usually have a simple shape. If the temperature is not as cold (around 15 degrees Fahrenheit), the crystals are larger and have a more complicated shape.

Dust may mingle with the water. The presence of dust also changes the size and shape of an ice crystal.

This image of a snow crystal was taken with a special microscope.

Kenneth G. Libbrecht

You can see the dust particles on this snowflake, which is shown under a powerful microscope.

Ice crystals contain a lot of information about their surroundings. This happens because of the special nature of water vapor. Water vapor clings to small **particles** in the air, such as dust or ash. When the vapor cools down and changes into liquid and then into ice, those particles are still part of the water. They are frozen into the ice crystals, too.

Snow can also catch tiny bubbles of air as it falls to Earth. Each bubble contains gases from the atmosphere, such as oxygen and carbon dioxide. The tiny gas bubbles and particles are all buried with the snow.

Scott Camazine/Alamy

Looking Closely at Snowflakes

You can examine snowflakes closely using a magnifying glass or a microscope. Most ice crystals have six sides. A snowflake can have up to 100 ice crystals. Scientists believe that no two snowflakes are alike. The temperature in the atmosphere and the presence of dust or ash affect the size and shape of ice crystals.

Bullet Rosette

Sectioned Plate

Capped Column

Simple Prisms

Double Plate

Fernlike Stellar Dendrite

Split Plate and Star

Hollow Column

Stellar Dendrite

Needle

Stellar Plate

Radiating Dendrite

Triangular Crystal

Rimmed Crystal

12-sided Snowflake

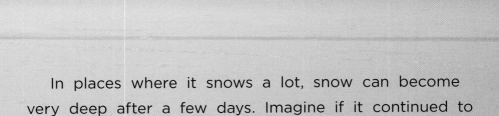

Snow and ice cover nearly 80 percent of Greenland.

In places where it snows a lot, snow can become very deep after a few days. Imagine if it continued to snow for thousands of years without melting away.

Each fresh layer of snow would press down on the older snow and pack it down. The frozen water, along with any dust, ash, or bubbles of gas that it clung to, would be **compacted** within the ice.

This is how ice built up in the polar regions. The ice in places such as Antarctica and Greenland formed over thousands of years. Dust, ash, and gases from thousands of years ago are also buried in the ice.

Peter Adams/JAI/CORBIS

❄ CHAPTER 3 ❄
Looking Closely at Ice

Scientists can learn what Earth's climate and atmosphere were like in the past by studying the layers of ancient ice in the polar regions. The particles of dust and the gas bubbles frozen with the snow change the **composition** of the ice layers.

Using a hollow drill, scientists extract a column of ice called an ice core. The drill has sharp teeth that spin and cut through the ice. If you twist and push a hollow tube down into soft snow, a column of snow fills up the inside of the tube. The drill works in exactly the same way: As it pushes down, the hollow part of the drill fills up with ice.

The Best Place to Drill

Before they extract the ice, scientists look for a place where the ice hasn't melted or moved much over a long period. It's also important that the ice doesn't have any crevasses, or deep cracks. The scientists test the ice right at the drilling site. They use radar to find out how deep the ice is and whether there are many layers beneath the surface.

This drill is used to extract ice cores in polar regions.

David Hay Jones/Photo Researchers, Inc

10

The ice core is removed in sections. After one section is extracted, the drill is put back into the same hole to bring up another section of older ice from lower down.

A typical section of ice is between 2 feet and 10 feet long. Although the sections are small, the full ice core could be about 300 feet long. This means that the scientists drilled 300 feet down into the ice! An ice core may be extracted from more than 2 miles down in polar regions where the ice is very thick.

ARCTIC IMAGES/Alamy

This scientist is holding up a section of ice core.

When a section of ice core is placed over a strong light, it's easier to see the layers in the ice.

When the ice cores have been extracted, the sections are sent to a laboratory, where they are studied carefully.

Scientists use a saw to cut the sections of ice core. Each core is sliced into smaller pieces so that scientists can run different tests on the same section of ice.

The scientists carefully **analyze** the sections of ice core using tools such as microscopes to magnify the tiny particles captured in the ice. They can identify changes in the ice from year to year. Ash and volcanic gases might show that a volcano erupted around the time an ice layer formed. Traces of salt might mean that windy storms blew in from the ocean.

Photograph by Kendrick Taylor, DRI, University of Nevada-Reno, NOAA/National Geophysical Data Center

The gas bubbles in the ice also hold clues to the past. Oxygen that is frozen into these bubbles tells us what the temperature of Earth was like at the time the ice formed.

Scientists also test the ice for gases such as carbon dioxide and methane. These are called "greenhouse gases" because they trap the sun's heat and keep it in Earth's atmosphere.

Knowing the amount of greenhouse gases in the atmosphere when the snow fell is yet another thing that allows scientists to figure out what temperatures were like in the past.

A scientist examines a thin section of an ice core.

The layers of crystals buried in ice cores are like a time line that shows changes in the climate. The information in the layers helps us learn what the climate was like in the past. It also provides information about weather patterns and can help scientists learn how these patterns have changed. Scientists can use this information to predict how Earth's climate might change in the future.

As a solid, liquid, or gas, water captures important information about the world around us. Who would have thought that ancient ice in Antarctica and Greenland could hold so many secrets about Earth's past? It's amazing how much we can learn when we know where to look and when we look closely.

This Antarctic glacier contains snow and ice that have built up over many years.

Summarize

Use the most important details from *Secrets of the Ice* to summarize the selection. Your graphic organizer may help.

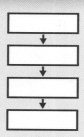

Text Evidence

1. What features on page 10 help you identify the kind of text *Secrets of the Ice* is? **GENRE**

2. How does the diagram on page 5 explain the way the water cycle works? **SEQUENCE**

3. What does the word *expand* mean on page 3? Use context clues to figure out its meaning and to find an antonym on the same page. **ANTONYMS**

4. Write about how information gets buried in the ice. What happens first, next, last? How do scientists get the information from the ice? Include details from the text in your answer. **WRITE ABOUT READING**

Compare Texts
Read about a girl who discovers that she can see things up close.

SUPER-VISION

Mia ate her breakfast and sighed heavily. All her friends were away on vacation, and she was bored.

"Cheer up!" said her mom. She wiped an eyelash off Mia's cheek. "Blow this and make a wish—that's what my grandmother used to say."

Mia blew the eyelash into the air, wishing, "Please let me see something NEW today!"

She opened her eyes and looked around. Her little brother, Ben, had spilled both salt and sugar on the table. As she looked at the gritty white crystals, Mia began to frown. The harder she stared, the bigger the crystals became. She realized they were different. The salt crystals were little cubes, while the sugar crystals were hexagonal shapes.

Mia blinked hard, and the crystals were tiny once more. She tried staring again. Sure enough, things magnified when she focused, and her vision returned to normal when she blinked.

"Mom," she said, "I have microscopic vision."

"That's nice," her mother replied distractedly.

Microscopic vision made ordinary things extraordinary. Mia spent quite some time examining the skin on her arm, looking at the tiny pores and hair follicles in minute detail.

"Earth to Mia! Come in, Mia!" called Mom. "Take the trash out, please. Now."

The front yard was a journey of discovery, filled with intriguing spiderwebs, leaves, and specks of dirt. Mia was looking at the world with new eyes.

In a happy daze, she lifted the lid of the trash can and then shrieked. It was like a scene from a horror movie! Rotten apples, blackened banana peels, moldy crusts! Who knew that old food could look so disgusting? Mia reeled away from the trash can and bolted over to Mom.

Mom was in the yard, and Ben was playing on the grass next to her. Mia's magnifying eyes zoomed in on a column of ugly monsters marching toward Ben's foot! Mia gasped.

"Mia!" said Mom. "What are you doing?"

Mia blinked, and the marching monsters transformed into a line of ants.

Mia caught a loose eyelash on Ben's cheek, closed her eyes, and blew it into the air. She wished: "Please give me back my normal eyesight!"

She opened her eyes and focused on Ben's hair. Nothing. Relieved, she kissed Ben's cheek.

"You're in a better mood," said Mom.

"Let's just say I'm seeing things in a whole new light!" replied Mia.

Make Connections

What does Mia discover about the world with her microscopic vision? **ESSENTIAL QUESTION**

How are the scientists in *Secrets of the Ice* similar to Mia in *Super-vision*? **TEXT TO TEXT**

Glossary

analyze *(AN-uh-lighz)* study or examine something closely *(page 12)*

atmosphere *(AT-muh-sfeer)* the layer of gases that surround Earth *(page 4)*

compacted *(kom-PAK-tuhd)* pressed together to become harder and take up less space *(page 9)*

composition *(kom-puh-ZI-shun)* all of the parts that something is made up of *(page 10)*

condense *(kun-DENS)* to change from a gas to a liquid as a result of cooling *(page 4)*

evaporation *(ee-va-puh-RAY-shuhn)* the process of water becoming a gas *(page 4)*

particles *(PAHR-ti-kuhlz)* tiny pieces *(page 7)*

solvent *(SAWL-vuhnt)* a liquid used for dissolving other substances *(page 3)*

states *(stayts)* forms or conditions of being *(page 2)*

Index

Antarctica, *9, 14*

freezing point, *3*

gases, *7, 9, 12, 13*

greenhouse gases, *13*

Greenland, *9, 14*

ice cores, *10–14*

ice crystals, *6–8*

precipitation, *5*

snowflakes, *6–8*

water cycle, *4, 5*

water vapor, *2–8*

Focus on Science

Purpose To create a mini water cycle

Procedure

You will need a large bowl, plastic wrap, a glass that is shorter than the bowl, water, and some coins.

Step 1 ▸ Pour the water into the bowl until it is about a quarter full.

Step 2 ▸ Put the glass in the center of the bowl.

Step 3 ▸ Cover the bowl tightly with plastic wrap. Set several coins in the center of the plastic so they are above the glass.

Step 4 ▸ Put the bowl on a sunny windowsill for a few days.

Conclusion What happened? Is the water level in the bowl the same? What changed with the glass? Why? The principles of the water cycle work in a mini cycle that you can make, as well as in the natural world around us.